Keep 'Em in STiTCHeS

"MY MEMORY'S NOT AS SHARP AS IT USED TO BE. AND...MY MEMORY'S NOT AS SHARP AS IT USED TO BE."

HoRACe VinSon

Evergreen PRESS

Keep 'Em in Stitches
by Horace Vinson
Copyright © 2009 Horace Vinson

ISBN 978-1-58169-335-5
For Worldwide Distribution
Printed in the U.S.A.

Evergreen Press
P.O. Box 191540 • Mobile, AL 36619
800-367-8203
www.evergreenpress.com

Table of Contents

Dedication

Dedicated to my wife of 50 years,
my children, grandchildren,
and all my friends—
both of them!

Introduction

Humor is a part of the spice of life. The Bible says that a merry heart does good like a medicine. There is a time to laugh and a time to cry. There are times we all need to lighten up and laugh a little. Laughter means to be amused. If you don't find this book funny, then try laughing at yourself, and you will never run out of amusement.

Just remember as you read this book, "Laughter is a fun thing to do." As you read the jokes, stories, and one-liners in this book, I hope you do so with an open mind. Although, if your mind is too open, your brain might fall out. I hope you proceed with caution and at your own risk!

A little old lady at the
bus stop asked, "Has the
next bus left yet?"

Senior Moments

An elderly couple had dinner at another couple's house. After the meal, the wives left the table and went into the kitchen. The two elderly gentlemen were talking, and one said, "Last night we went out to a new restaurant, and it was really great. I would recommend it very highly." The other man said, "What's the name of the restaurant?" The first man thought and thought, and finally asked, "What's the name of the flower you give to someone you love? You know...the one that is red and has thorns." "Do you mean a rose?" "Yes," the man said. He turned toward the kitchen and yelled, "Rose, what's the name of that restaurant we went to last night?"

Getting old is when your toupee looks good, your false teeth work fine, your peg leg is O.K., but you sure do miss your mind.

An old fellow got up from the couch and told his wife he was going to get some ice cream. She said, "Bring me some and put chocolate on it." He came back with plain toast and she said, "Didn't I tell you to put jelly on it?"

As we get older, we need to stay in shape. My grandmother started walking five miles a day when she was 60. Now she's 97, and we don't know where she is!

A little old lady in New York called 911 and said, "There's a burglar in my house!" The dispatcher asked, "What's your address?" The little old lady replied, "I'd better not tell you, I don't want to get involved."

Three sisters—ages 92, 94, and 96—lived in a house together. One night the 96 year old drew a bath. She put her foot in and paused. She yelled to the other sisters, "Was I getting in or out of the bath?" The 94 year old yelled back, "I don't know. I'll come up and see." She started up the stairs and paused, "Was I going up the stairs or down?" The 92 year old was sipping her tea at the kitchen table, listening to her sisters. She shook her head and said, "I sure hope I never get that forgetful." She knocked on wood for good measure. She then yelled, "I'll come up and help both of you as soon as I see who's at the door."

My memory is so bad that I finally have a clear conscience!

A senior citizen was driving down the freeway when his cell phone rang. Answering, he heard his wife's voice urgently warning him, "Herman, I just heard on the news that there's a car going the wrong way on Interstate 77. Please be careful!" "Heck," said Herman, "It's not just one car. It's hundreds of them!"

My senior moments sometimes turn into a week long vacation!

The nice thing about
being senile is that you can hide
your own Easter eggs.

An elderly Floridian called 911 on her cell phone to report that her car had been broken into. She was hysterical as she explained her situation to the dispatcher, "They've stolen the stereo, the steering wheel, the brake pedal, and even the accelerator!" The dispatcher said, "Stay calm. An officer is on the way." A few minutes later, the officer radioed in, "Disregard the 911 call. She got in the back seat by mistake."

Two old men were sitting on a park bench. One said to the other, "Refresh my memory. Was it you or your brother that died in World War II?"

Uncle George is so forgetful that he can play hide and seek all by himself.

Two elderly women had been friends for many decades. Over the years, they had shared all kinds of activities and adventures. Lately, their activities had been limited to meeting a few times a week to play cards. One day, they were playing cards when one looked at the other and said, "Now don't get mad at me…I know we've been friends for a long time, but I just can't think of your name! I've thought and thought, but I can't remember it. Please tell me what your name is." For at least three minutes, her friend just stared and glared at her. Finally, she said, "How soon do you need to know?"

My secrets are safe with my friends—they can't remember them either.

The Senility Prayer:
Grant me the senility to forget the people I never knew, the good fortune to meet those I do, and the vision to tell the difference.

As I get older, the more notes I need.

You Know You Are Getting Older When:

- The gleam in your eye is from the sun hitting your bifocals.

- Your children begin to look middle-aged.

- You know all the answers, but nobody is asking you any questions.

- Dialing long distance wears you out.

- You look forward to a dull evening.

- You burn the midnight oil after nine o'clock.

- Your knees buckle, but your belt won't.

- You turn out the lights for economic reasons rather than romantic ones.

- You feel like the morning after, but you haven't been anywhere the night before.

- You bend over to pick up something and wonder if you can make the round trip.

WORDS OF WISDOM

We do not stop laughing because we grow old; we grow old because we stop laughing!

These days about half the
stuff in my shopping cart says,
"For fast relief!"

Not Getting Any Younger

As we get older, we tend to slow down. One day a man stepped on a snail, and his friend asked him why he did that. He said, "That thing has been following me around all day long."

<hr />

A man went to the doctor. The doc examined him and said, "The best I can tell you is that you have ten left." The man asked, "How many? Ten years, ten months, ten weeks, or ten days?" The doc replied, "Nine, eight, seven, six, five, four, three..."

<hr />

Another elderly man went to the doctor with a banana in his ear and a pickle up his nose. The doctor said to him, "I'll tell you right now, you're not eating right."

This old fellow who could not read or write went to a bank to cash a check. The bank teller asked him to sign the check. He said, "I can't write." She told him, "Just put an 'X' on the check." He put a big 'X' on it and then a little 'x' next to it. The teller said, "I understand the big 'X' but what is the little one for?" "Oh," he said, "I'm a junior."

A 91-year-old man got married. His friend asked him, "Is she a good cook?" He replied, "No." The friend asked, "Is she good looking?" He said, "No." Then the friend asked, "Is she rich?" He said, "No." Exasperated, the friend demanded, "Well, why in the world did you get married?" He replied, "She can drive at night."

I used to eat a lot of natural foods until I learned that most people die of natural causes.

A preacher visited an elderly woman in the nursing home, and while talking with her he began to eat some peanuts in a bowl by her bed. After a while, he noticed he had eaten nearly all of her peanuts, so he apologized and told her he would bring some more the next visit. She said, "That's quite all right, sonny, it's all I can do to suck the chocolate off them."

~~~

My idea of weight lifting is standing up.

~~~

Old Folks Party Games:

- Musical recliners.
- Spin the bottle of Mylanta.
- Simon says something incoherent.
- Red rover, red rover, the nurse says bend over.
- Twenty questions shouted into your good ear.
- Pin the toupee on the bald guy.

~~~

God put me on earth to accomplish a number of things. Right now, I'm so far behind that I think I'll live forever.

Any day above ground is a good day.

Boudreaux and Thibodeaux, who were greeters at the local Wal-Mart, were taking a break. Boudreaux said, "Man, this old age is terrible. I ache all over." Thibodeaux said, "Not me, man, I feel like a newborn baby—no hair, no teeth, I'm hungry, and I think I just soiled my pants."

One old guy told another that he had a frog that could talk. If you kissed it, it would turn into a beautiful princess and say sweet things. The other man took the frog, put it in his pocket, and said, "At my age I'd rather have a talking frog than a pretty princess."

Two men were walking down the streets of heaven. One said, "You know, if we hadn't eaten so much oatmeal we could have been here ten years ago!"

A widow went to a nursing home, saw a man, and said, "You look like my third husband." He said, "How many times have you been married?" She said, "Twice."

Two older women were talking. One said to the other, "One of us should go on to heaven, then I could move in with my daughter."

Little Johnny said, "My Uncle George is real consistent. He goes to the bathroom every morning at 7 a.m. The problem is he doesn't get up until 9 a.m."

I knew I was getting older when I realized the little old gray-headed lady I was helping across the street was my wife.

A ninety-one-year-old man went to his doctor for a checkup. The doctor examined him and sent him home. The next day the doctor was driving to work and saw the old man jogging down the street with a beautiful young woman, and they were laughing and having a good time. The doctor pulled over to the curb and asked, "Man, what are you doing out here like this?" The old man said, "Doc, I'm just doing what you told me. You said for me to get a hot mama and be cheerful." The doc shook his head and replied, "No, no I didn't. I told you that you had a heart murmur and to be careful!"

I hear snap, crackle, and pop at breakfast, but I'm not eating cereal.

The Benefits of Growing Older:

- Kidnappers are not very interested in you.

- In a hostage situation, you are likely to be released first.

- No one expects you to run into a burning building.

- People call at 9 p.m. and ask, "Did I wake you?"

- People no longer view you as a hypochondriac.

- There's nothing left to learn the hard way.

- Things you buy now won't wear out.

- You can eat dinner at four o'clock.

- You enjoy hearing about other people's operations.

- You get into a heated argument about pension plans.

- You and your teeth don't sleep together anymore.

- You can sing along with the elevator music.

- Your eyes won't get much worse.

- You no longer think of speed limits as a challenge.

- You have a party, and the neighbors don't even realize it.

- You quit trying to hold your stomach in, no matter who walks in the room.

- Your investment in health insurance is finally beginning to pay off.

- Your joints are more accurate than the National Weather Service.

- Your supply of brain cells is finally down to a manageable size.

A 60-year-old man said to his friend, "I think I'll live to be 120." The other man asked, "Why do you say that?" He said, "Well, I'm half-dead now."

⌇⌇⌇

Just before the funeral services, the undertaker went up to the very elderly widow and asked, "How old was your husband?" "Ninety-eight," she replied, "Two years older than me." "So, you're ninety-six," the undertaker commented. She responded, "Hardly worth going back home, is it?"

⌇⌇⌇

Reporters, interviewing a 104-year-old woman: "And what do you think is the best thing about being 104?" the reporter asked. The old woman replied, "No peer pressure."

⌇⌇⌇

I've sure gotten old! I've had two bypass surgeries, a hip replacement, and new knees. I fought prostate cancer and diabetes. I'm half-blind, can't hear anything quieter than a jet engine, take forty different medications that make me dizzy, winded, and subject to blackouts. I've had bouts with dementia, have poor circulation, and can hardly feel my hands and feet anymore. I can't remember if I'm 85 or 92. I've lost all my friends. But, thank God, I still have my driver's license!

I feel like my body has gotten totally out of shape, so I got my doctor's permission to join a fitness club and start exercising. I decided to take an aerobic class for seniors. I bent, twisted, gyrated, jumped up and down, and perspired for almost an hour. And by the time I got my leotards on, the class was over!

An elderly woman decided to prepare her will and told her preacher that she had two final requests: first, she wanted to be cremated; and second, she wanted her ashes scattered over the Wal-Mart parking lot. "Wal-Mart!" the preacher exclaimed, "why Wal-Mart?" She answered, "Then I'll be sure my daughters visit me at least twice a week!"

Do you want to know how to prevent sagging? Just eat until the wrinkles fill out.

I'm not going bald; I'm just growing through my hair.

It's scary when you start making the same noises as your coffee maker.

I get up in the morning and dust off my wits.
I pick up the paper and read the obits.
If my name is not there, I know I'm not dead,
so I eat a good breakfast and go back to bed.

The old comedian opened his monologue with the words, "It's good to be here. Hey, at my age, it's good to be anywhere!"

I can tell I am getting older because it takes longer to rest than to get tired!

~

When you're 30 years old, you worry about what people think about you. When you're 40 years old, you no longer care what they think. By the time you're 50, you realize no one was thinking about you in the first place.

~

WORDS OF WISDOM

The only thing worse than losing your sight is losing your vision.

Laughter is a fix that will fix the fix that you are in or are fixin' to be in.

Fear knocked, Faith answered, and there was no one there.

Golfer to Caddy: "Boy, I've never played this badly before." Caddy: "Oh, so you've played before."

Fore!

A woman killed an intruder with a golf club. The investigator asked her, "How many times did you hit him?" She said, "Nine, but put me down for a five."

〜〜〜

A preacher was playing golf, and every time he would hit a bad shot he'd say, "boulder, boulder." After a while his playing partner said, "I don't understand why every time you hit a bad shot you say, 'boulder.'" The preacher explained, "That's the biggest dam I can think of."

〜〜〜

One beautiful day Charles and Billy were playing golf when Charles hit a bad slice deep into the woods. He grabbed an eight iron and headed for the woods to look for his ball. As he was looking through the brush and tall grass, he spotted something shiny.

Looking closer he saw an eight iron lying in the grass next to a skeleton. He called out to Billy, "Come here quickly—we have big trouble here." Billy called out, "What's the matter, Charles?" Charles said, "Bring me my seven iron. It looks like you can't get out of here with an eight iron."

A couple was having some marriage problems, and they were talking with the pastor. After the counseling session the pastor walked over, hugged the wife, and said, "This is what she needs every day." The husband said, "Pastor, I can only bring her in on Mondays and Thursdays because I play golf the other days."

A man came home from a golf game one day, threw his clubs in the corner, and said, "I'm not playing golf with Fred anymore." His wife asked, "Why not?" He said, "Would you play golf with someone who moves his ball around, cheats on the score card, and fusses all the time?" She said, "No, I wouldn't." He said, "Neither will Fred."

Fore!

One golfer said to another, "I have to putt from memory." The other golfer asked, "Why do you say that?" "Well," he said, patting his oversized stomach, "When I put the ball where I can see it, I can't reach it; and when I put the ball where I can reach it, I can't see it."

Golfer: "Excuse me, would you mind if I play through? I've just heard that my wife has been taken seriously ill."

One woman said to her neighbor, "I just got a new set of golf clubs for my husband." The other lady replied, "I'd say that was a good trade."

Two golfers were on the first tee. The first one hit the ball. It went over the fence, across the ditch, hit a tire on a bus, and bounced back onto the fairway. The other golfer looked at him and said, "Man, how did you do that?" First golfer said, "You have to know the bus schedule."

Some Catholics and Jews decided to have a golf tournament. The Catholics said, "Let's ordain Jack Nicklaus as a priest so we can win." They played, but the Jews won. The Catholics said, "We could have won if it hadn't been for Rabbi Woods."

Golfer to Caddy: If I keep playing this bad, I think I will drown myself.
Caddy: I don't think you can keep your head down long enough.

One golfer to another: "Man, you sure have a good short game. Too bad it's off the tee."

I told my golfing buddy that it's good to be on the green side of the grass.

Golf is an ineffectual endeavor to put an insignificant object into an obscure hole with completely inadequate instruments.

Fore!

Three retirees, each with a hearing loss, were playing golf one fine March day. One remarked to the other, "Windy, isn't it?" "No," the second man replied, "It's Thursday." And the third man chimed in, "So am I. Let's get a Coke."

***

WORDS OF WISDOM

A smile is a curve that sets a lot of things straight.

Laughter is the shortest distance between two people.

If you aim at nothing, you will hit it every time.

Do you remember...
lemonade stands?

The Good Ole Days

Things Ain't What They Used To Be

Remember...

• Sittin' on the porch.

• Simon says, "Kick the can."

• Red light, green light.

• Penny candy from the corner store.

• Hopscotch, butterscotch, and skates with keys.

• Jacks, kickball, and dodge ball.

• Mother may I?

• Hula hoops.

• Coke bottles with the names of cities on the bottom.

- Catching lightning bugs in a jar.

- Playing slingshot.

- Backyard shows.

- Cops and robbers.

- Laughing so hard that your stomach hurts.

- When it took five minutes for the TV to warm up.

- When nobody owned a purebred dog.

- When a quarter was a decent allowance and another quarter a huge bonus.

- When you got your windshield cleaned, oil checked, and gas pumped.

- When they threatened to keep kids back a grade if they failed...and did!

- When being sent to the principal's office was nothing compared to the fate that awaited a misbehaving student at home.

- When a '57 Chevy was everyone's dream car to cruise the strip, peel out, lay rubber, or watch submarine races.

- When people went steady and girls wore a class ring with an inch of wrapped dental floss coated with pastel frosted nail polish so it would fit her finger.

Do you ever wonder why we park on the driveway and drive on the parkway?

WORDS OF WISDOM
Life is like a roll of toilet paper—the closer it gets to the end, the faster it goes.

A day of worry burns more energy than a week's work.

Psalms 2:4—He who sits in the heavens laughs.

There are 156 different sins.
One pastor has already received
40 requests for the list!

Preachers

One preacher had a bicycle, rode it down the street, and saw a boy with a lawn mower. The preacher said, "I need a lawn mower, and you need a bicycle—why don't we swap?" So they did. Later the boy was riding his bicycle down the street, saw the preacher pulling on the mower, and he couldn't get it to start. The boy said, "If you'll cuss it, it'll crank." The preacher said, "Son, I'm a preacher. I forgot how to cuss a long time ago." The boy said, "Just keep pulling, and it'll come back to you."

~~~~~~

The pastor was preaching his last sermon at a church, and afterward he was at the door greeting everyone. One little lady came up, shook his hand, and said, "I'm so sorry we're losing you." The preacher said, "That's all right; they'll send you a good one next time." The little lady replied, "Oh, they won't either. That's what they said the last time."

The blonde laughed out loud one Sunday as the preacher was speaking. Afterward the preacher asked her what she was laughing about. She said, "Well, I usually start telling myself jokes to keep me awake while you preach. This morning I heard one that I had never heard before."

~~~~~~

A preacher was to speak on tithing the following Sunday, so he came down early in the week and ran some wires down the pews attached to three buttons on the pulpit. When he got up to preach he said, "If you want to give 10 percent, stand up." Then he pushed the first button, and the people on the first three rows jumped to their feet.

Next he said, "If you want to give 20 percent, stand up." He pushed the second button, and the people on the next two rows jumped up.

Finally he said, "If you want to give 30 percent, stand up." He pushed the third button, and two people on the back row jumped up.

After the service, two deacons were found electrocuted on the back row.

A young man was called to preach, so he went to the bookstore to buy a Bible. When the clerk showed him a real nice, small Bible, he said, "No, I want a large one. I can preach through that little one in no time."

A country preacher said, "Bubba, please lead us in prayer." Three men and two women stood up.

One pastor received a call at 2 a.m. "Come over, help, we can't sleep." "What can I do at 2 a.m.?" "You could preach to us some."

A religious awakening is what takes place when the preacher gets through preaching.

One church member said to another, "I would rather hear our pastor preach than eat." The other one said, "Me too. I've heard him eat."

Pointing his finger at the congregation, the preacher said, "All you hypocrites who are snuff dippers, pipe smokers, liars, and drunkards, I hope your tongue sticks to the roooooooof of your mouth."

Ｏ ～～～～ Ｏ

A preacher awoke one morning to find a dead donkey in his front yard. He had no idea how it got there, but he knew he had to get rid of it. So he called the sanitation department, the health department, and several other agencies, but nobody seemed to care.

In desperation, the good reverend called the mayor and asked what could be done. The mayor must have been having a bad day. "Why bother me?" he asked. "You're a clergyman. It's your job to bury the dead." The pastor lost his cool, "Yes," he snapped, "but I thought I should at least notify the next of kin first."

Ｏ ～～～～ Ｏ

A man went to sleep every time the preacher started to speak. The preacher told the man's wife, "Why don't you wake him up?" The wife said, "You wake him up; you put him to sleep."

A preacher, a lawyer, and a doctor went deer hunting together. They got into the woods and all of a sudden, a big buck came right across in front of them. They all shot and the deer went down. When they got to the deer, they began to argue about who had killed it.

About that time, a game warden came up and said, "I'll examine the deer and settle this argument." After looking closely at the carcass he said, "The preacher shot the deer." They began to question him about how he could tell. He said, "Because the bullet went in one ear and out the other."

A little boy was standing in the hallway of the church, looking at a plaque on the wall. He asked the preacher what it meant. The preacher said, "Son, that is the list of names of men who died in the service." Scared, the boy asked, "Preacher, was it the morning or evening service?"

A pastor, feeling good about the sermon he had just preached, asked his wife, "How many great preachers preached today?" His wife answered, "One less than you think."

A pastor's daughter noticed that her father always bowed his head right before he preached. "I do that to ask the Lord to help me preach a good sermon." His daughter replied, "How come He doesn't do it?"

A pastor, presiding at the funeral of a woman who had been married four times, described the husbands. "The first husband was a banker; the second, a circus performer; the third, a preacher; and the fourth, an undertaker. One for the money, two for the show, three to get ready, and four to go."

A man called the church office and asked the secretary if the head hog of the trough was there. She answered, "I'm sorry, sir, but that is a very disrespectful thing to say about our pastor." The man replied, "That's all right, I was going to donate $5,000 to your building fund." The secretary said, "Wait just a minute, sir. I think I hear the pig coming down the hall now."

An Episcopalian priest and an Assembly of God pastor went to heaven. St. Peter told them to walk around on the streets of gold and make themselves at home. "But," he said, "do not make any racket when you pass the double doors." They asked, "Why?" He said, "That room is full of Baptists, and they think they're the only ones here."

A deacon said to his pastor after a Sunday morning service, "Pastor, your sermon was warm and moving—you were blowing a lot of hot air, and I was moved to take a nap."

A pastor told another pastor, "Our church was comfortably filled Sunday. There was plenty of room for everyone to lie down without kicking each other."

One baby cried out in church. The pastor reassured the mother, "That's all right; it doesn't bother me." The mother said, "Yes, but you're bothering him."

※ ～～ ※

Pastor to farmer: "If you had two farms, would you give me one?"

Farmer: "Sure I would, I only wish I had two so I could give you one."

Pastor: "If you had $10,000, would you give $1,000 to the Lord?"

Farmer: "Sure, I would love to give that."

Pastor: "If you had two pigs, would you give one to the Lord?"

Farmer: "Aw, that's not fair; you know I got two pigs."

※ ～～ ※

A pastor said of his congregation, "They give until it hurts, but they have a very low pain threshold. Some of them have an impediment in their reach, and a lot of them have sclerosis of the giver."

※ ～～ ※

This Mississippi man decided to visit mega churches across the country. He visited one that had a pay phone in the lobby with a sign that said, "Direct Line to God—$25,000." He visited a couple of other churches with the same sign but the amounts were $15,000. He made his way back to Mississippi and saw a phone in the lobby with a sign that said, "Direct Line to God—35 cents." He asked the pastor why the amount was so small. The pastor replied, "From here, it's a local call."

There is the story of a pastor who got up one Sunday and announced to his congregation, "I have good news and bad news. The good news is we have enough money to pay for our new building program. The bad news is it's still out there in your pockets."

WORDS OF WISDOM
The best sermons are lived, not preached.

It is logistically, biologically, and scientifically impossible to hear while you are talking. God gave us two ears and one mouth so we can listen twice as much as we talk.

Why did the blonde collect burned out light bulbs? So she could use them in her dark room!

Blondes Have More Fun

A farmer and his son came to town, which they hardly ever did except on special occasions. This time they went into the lobby of a fine hotel. They saw two shiny doors open. An old lady, overweight and in a wheelchair, entered the door to a little room. The doors closed, and they saw the numbers above the doorway flash on and off all in a row up to twelve where the light stayed on for awhile.

After a while, they saw the lights flash on and off from twelve back down to number one. When the doors opened, a very beautiful blonde walked out. Surprised, the two looked at each other, and the dad said to the son, "Go quickly and get your mama."

One blonde bought a puzzle, stayed up all night, and put it together. She thought she was extra smart because she finished it so quickly. The box had written on it: "for 3-5 years."

Another blonde was on the plane in the first-class section when the flight attendant told her that her ticket was for the regular passenger section. She told him, "I'm a blonde, I'm beautiful, I'm going to New York, and I'm not moving."

The flight attendant went and told the captain that the woman would not move, so he said, "I'm married to a blonde; I'll talk to her." He went back and whispered something in her ear. Immediately she got up and said, "Why didn't someone tell me this?"

The flight attendant was amazed at how quickly the woman changed seats, so he asked the captain what he had told her. The captain said that he told the blonde the first-class section was not going to New York.

Some blonde who had never ridden a horse finally got up enough courage to mount one. It took off and she fell off immediately and caught her foot in the stirrup. It probably would have hurt her badly if the Wal-Mart manager had not come and unplugged it.

A blonde bought an AM radio and had it six months before she knew she could play it at night.

A blonde said to another, "The Lord made us beautiful and dumb." "How's that?" the other woman asked. "Beautiful so men would love us, and dumb so we could love them."

A blonde and her football fanatic boyfriend went to a football game. On the way home the boyfriend asked, "Well, how did you like your first football game?" The blonde said, "Well, I really didn't understand it. When the game started, they tossed the coin to see who was going to get the 25 cents and then they spent the rest of the game yelling, 'Get the quarter back!'"

Did you hear about the blonde mortician? A woman went to the funeral home and found that the mortician had dressed her deceased husband in a black suit. She told the blonde mortician that she wanted him buried in a blue suit, and gave her a blank check, saying that money was no object. "Buy him the best suit possible."

She went back the next day to find her husband dressed in the blue suit; and the blonde mortician gave the woman back her check. When questioned, the mortician said, "The suit will not cost you anything. Another woman brought her husband in dressed in a blue suit and said just to make him look nice." The woman said, "So you just swapped the suits?" "No," the blonde mortician answered. "I just swapped their heads."

WORDS OF WISDOM

If we will learn to laugh at ourselves, we will always find something to make us happy.

Don't suppress laughter; it will go down inside you and spread out your hips.

Nonsense Mind Bogglers

• Which had you rather do or ride a bicycle?

• Did you bring your lunch or walk to work?

• Did you know it is faster to New York than it is by bus?

• What is the difference between a lemon?

• What is the length of a short piece of rope?

• If I've said anything I'm sorry for, I'm glad I said it.

❧

When the clock was first invented, how did they know what time to set it to?

❧

A man on the subway asked the person next to him, "Where is Pennsylvania Avenue?" The person replied, "You just watch me and get off just before I do."

❧

I wake up looking like my driver's license picture.

NASCAR: Non-Athletic Sport Centered Around Rednecks

Rednecks & Good Ole Boys

An old fellow was being interviewed on a radio program. He was asked what was the greatest invention ever invented. "Well, I think the car was the greatest thing that man ever came up with. You used to have to walk or ride a mule everywhere you went."

The next fellow was asked the same question. He said, "The airplane is the greatest invention because you can get on it and go all over the world nowadays."

The next old country fellow was asked the same question. And he said, "The thermos bottle was the greatest thing that was ever made." The interviewer asked why he thought that. And the old boy replied, "Well, you can put something in it one morning hot, and it will keep it hot all day. Then the next day you can put something in it cold, and it will keep it cold all day." Then the interviewer said, "What's so special about that?" He said, "How does it know?"

The country boy got a job in the city. He thought group insurance meant the whole group had to get sick before you could collect.

***

A duck hunter had a dog that he was very proud of, so he asked his neighbor to come over for a demonstration. He would shoot a duck, and the dog would walk across the water and bring back the duck. He did this several times, and the neighbor didn't seem to be impressed at all. He said, "That dog can't swim, can he?"

***

A man in town was very slow; you might say his elevator didn't go all the way to the top floor. The town council felt sorry for him and gave him the job of shining the cannon that was down at the square. He worked hard at it for a number of months. Then he came in one day and said, "I quit."

The council said, "We thought you were doing a good job." He replied, "Yes, I been workin' hard and savin' my money. I finally decided to buy my own cannon and go into business for myself."

Two factory workers were in the office talking about the stupid men they had working for them. One said, "I'll show you just how stupid some of them are." He called one of his men to the office, gave him a quarter, and told him to go and buy him a new Cadillac.

The worker took the quarter and went outside. The other foreman said, "That's nothing compared to one of *my* men." So he called his man to the office and told him to go down to the bowling alley and see if he was there.

So that worker went outside and started talking with the first worker. The first worker said, "My boss is so stupid, he gave me this quarter and told me to go buy him a new Cadillac. He knew all the time that I couldn't drive."

The other one said, "That's nothing. My boss told me to go down to the bowling alley to see if he's down there, and all he would have to do is to pick up the phone and call down there to see for himself."

A boy was late for work one morning; the boss asked him what the problem was. The boy said that the bathroom caught fire. The boss asked, "Well, did it burn the rest of the house?" The boy said, "No, but it would have if the garden hadn't gotten in the way."

<hr />

A squirrel hunter in the woods came upon another hunter who had squirrels tied all over him. He asked him, "How in the world did you get that many squirrels? I've been out here all day and don't even have one."

The hunter said, "Well, you can see that I'm real ugly, so what I do is get two rocks and rub them together. When the squirrels look at me, they have a heart attack and fall over so all I have to do is pick them up."

"Well, you're not nearly as ugly as a woman I saw sitting in a truck at the edge of the woods." The man said, "Oh, that's my wife. She used to hunt with me, but it got to where she tore them up too bad to eat so now she just waits in the truck."

<hr />

This guy bought two tickets to a football game. His buddy asked, "Why did you buy two tickets?" He said, "Well, I know that during the game I'll get rowdy and cause a scene, and they'll throw me out. I'm gonna use this other ticket to get back in."

Leroy: "What are you doing?"
Darrell: "I'm writing a letter to a friend."
Leroy: "Don't try to fool me. You can't write."
Darrell: "That's all right. He can't read either."

A city boy went out west to become a cowboy. His friend saw him and said, "You're putting that saddle on backwards." The city boy said, "Don't be so sure. How do you know which way I am going?"

Boudreaux said to Thibodeaux, "I got me a good recommendation from my last boss." Thibodeaux asked, "Yeah, what was it?" Boudreaux replied, "He told my new boss if he could get me to work for him, he would be doing well."

There was a country boy who went out and made his mark on the world, and now he wants to learn how to write his full name.

A man woke up in the night and heard burglars in the house. He shouted, "What's going on here?" The burglars replied, "We're looking for money." The man said, "Well, turn on the light, and I'll help you look."

Boudreaux said to Thibodeaux, "I used to snore so loudly that I kept myself awake, but I solved the problem." Thibodeaux asked, "What did you do?" Boudreaux said, "I started sleeping in the next room."

Two ole country boys wanted to learn how to fly. They finally got their pilots' license and went up for a ride. After enjoying the time in the air, they came in for a rough landing. One said, "Man, did you see how short that landing strip was?" The other replied, "Yeah, but look how wide it is!"

Cecil's Uncle Henry won the lottery up in Ozark, Arkansas. He gets three dollars a year for a million years!

When I was growing up, we lived so far out in the country that nobody lived behind us.

Boudreaux and Thibodeaux got a contract to fix the levees in New Orleans. When they got through, the inspector went out to look. They had put up a hurricane chain-link fence across it.

Boudreaux went to the store to buy some two-by-fours. The clerk asked him, "How long do you want them?" Boudreaux said, "A long time."

Boudreaux and Thibodeaux were downtown one day, and Boudreaux said, "Let's go on this economy cruise for $29.95." So they went in and paid their money. The cruise people called Boudreaux in for an interview. When he entered the room, he was jumped on, beat up, bound up, and thrown through a trap door into the bayou.

Then it came time for Thibodeaux to go in for an interview. He was also jumped on, beat up, bound up, and thrown into a trap door into the bayou.

Down in the bayou, Thibodeaux looked at Boudreaux and said, "Do you think they'll feed us good on this cruise?" Boudreaux replied, "I don't know; they didn't last year."

~~~

While driving in Pennsylvania, a family caught up with an Amish carriage. The owner of the carriage obviously had a sense of humor. Attached to the back of the carriage was a hand printed sign that read, "Energy efficient vehicle: runs on oats and grass. Caution: Do not step in exhaust."

~~~

A man who was not the smartest person in town was hired by the city public works department and given the job of painting the white lines down the streets.

He went to work and did pretty well the first day. The next day he didn't get quite as far, and then the next day he didn't get far at all.

His boss called him in and asked him why he was getting less and less done every day. His reply was, "Well, I keep getting farther and farther from my paint bucket."

WORDS OF WISDOM

An optimist is one who takes a frying pan on a fishing trip.

If you want someone to laugh at your jokes, tell them they have a good sense of humor.

If Satan knocks on your door, ask Jesus if He will get the door for you.

Old man: "My best friends are medical people."

Shrinks and Docs

A woman went to the psychiatrist and told him that her husband had a problem—he thought he was a refrigerator. "That's not so bad; that's really a harmless thing," the psychiatrist told her. "Well, maybe," said the woman, "but he sleeps with his mouth open, and the light keeps me awake."

A woman in a psychiatrist's office said, "I think all the time that I am a pair of curtains." The doctor said, "Stop worrying and pull yourself together."

A lady went to a doctor for a checkup. The doctor asked, "How much do you weigh?" She said, "115 pounds." She stepped on the scale and weighed 140 pounds. The doctor asked, "How tall are you?" She said, "5'8"." He measured her and she was 5'2". He then said, "Let me check your blood pressure." He checked and said, "My goodness, your blood pressure is very high." She replied, "It's no wonder. I came in here tall and skinny, and now I'm short and fat."

A man said to a psychiatrist, "I have two problems. Number one, I feel like I'm a Pepsi machine." The psychiatrist said, "No, you're not a Pepsi machine." So they argued back and forth. The psychiatrist said, "What is your number two problem?" He said, "I'm out of order."

A doctor told a man that his leg was swollen, but he shouldn't worry about it. The man said, "No, if your leg was swollen, I wouldn't worry about it either."

Hello! Welcome to the Psychiatric Hotline:

• If you are obsessive-compulsive,
   please press 1 repeatedly.

- If you are co-dependent, please ask someone else to press 2.

- If you have multiple personalities, please press 3, 4, 5, and 6.

- If you are paranoid/delusional, we know who you are and what you want, so please remain on the line until we can trace your call.

- If you are schizophrenic, listen closely and a little voice will tell you which number to press.

- If you are manic-depressive, it doesn't matter which number you press—no one will answer.

***

Boudreaux went to his doctor for a checkup. A couple of days later, the doctor called him up and said, "I've got some good news and some bad news." Boudreaux said, "Give me the good news first." The doc said, "You have 24 hours to live." Boudreaux replied, "If that's the good news, what's the bad news?" The doc said, "I tried to reach you yesterday."

***

A lady came in to see the counselor and said, "I have half a mind to get married." The counselor said, "That's all it takes. When are you thinking about getting married?" She said, "Constantly."

A woman came in for counseling. She said she thought her husband was a chicken. The counselor said, "He needs to come in; he needs help. And by the way, I'll need to see some of the eggs too."

This doctor used to operate only on midgets. He had to quit—he ran short on patients.

A man hated his dentist because he was always looking down in the mouth.

The baby was so ugly when he was born, the doctor spanked the mama!

True story: Two old men were sitting in the VA clinic. One said to the other, "When I got out of the Army, they gave me a 10% disability for being crazy, and you know, last year the Lord really blessed me. They upped my disability to 50%."

WORDS OF WISDOM
It's been proven that if you can't take a joke, you will have to take medicine.

A merry heart does good like a medicine, so when you laugh, it does your heart good. That's why humor is good just for the health of it.

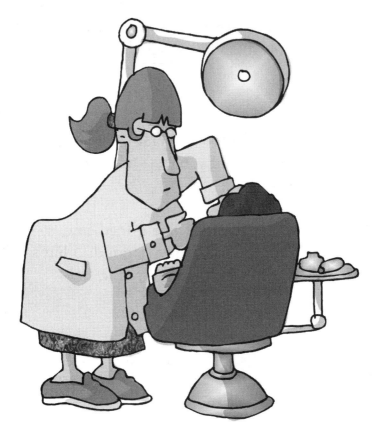

The Dentist's Hymn...
"Crown Him With Many Crowns"

Favorite Hymns

The Weatherman's Hymn .... "There Shall Be Showers of Blessing"

The Contractor's Hymn .... "The Church's One Foundation"

The Golfer's Hymn .... "There Is a Green Hill Far Away"

The Optometrist's Hymn .... "Open My Eyes That I Might See"

Realtor's Hymn .... "I've Got a Mansion Over the Hilltop"

The Politician's Hymn .... "Standing on the Promises"

The Tailor's Hymn .... "Holy, Holy, Holy"

The IRS Agent's Hymn .... "I Surrender All"

The Gossip's Hymn .... "Pass It On"

The Electrician's Hymn .... "Send the Light"

The Shopper's Hymn .... "Sweet Buy and Buy"

Speeder's Highway Hymns:

45 mph ...."God Will Take Care of You"

55 mph ...."Guide Me, O Thou Great Jehovah"

65 mph ...."Nearer My God to Thee"

75 mph ...."Nearer Still Nearer"

85 mph ...."This World Is Not My Home"

95 mph ...."Lord, I'm Coming Home"

100+ mph ...."Precious Memories"

The Way We Might Really Sing Hymns If We Were Being Honest!

I Surrender Some
(Instead of ALL)

There Shall Be Sprinkles of Blessing
(Instead of SHOWERS)

Fill My Spoon, Lord
(Instead of CUP)

Oh, How I Like Jesus
(Instead of LOVE)

He's Quite a Bit to Me
(Instead of IS ALL THE WORLD)

I Love To Talk About Telling the Story
(Instead of TELL)

Take My Life and Let Me Be
(Instead of IT BE)

It Is My Secret What God Can Do
(Instead of IT IS NO SECRET)

Onward, Christian Reserves
(Instead of SOLDIERS)

Where He Leads Me, I Will Consider Following
(Instead of I WILL FOLLOW)

Just As I Pretend To Be
(Instead of I AM)

When the Saints Go Sneaking In
(Instead of MARCHING IN)

WORDS OF WISDOM

Life is like an ice cream cone. You get it licked on one side, and it runs down on the other.

We need to get serious about this laughter business.

Signs of the Times

Sign on a fence:
Salesmen welcome, dog food
is expensive.

Taxidermist's window:
We really know our stuff.

On a front door:
Everyone here is a vegetarian
—except for the dog.

Car dealership:
The best way to get back on your feet
is to miss a car payment.

Optometrist's office:
If you don't see what you're looking
for, you're in the right place.

A camel is a racehorse
that's been put together by
a church committee.

Church Folk

A Mennonite man was milking his cow when the cow hauled off and kicked him. He looked the cow right in the eye and said, "Thou knowest that I can't cuss thee; thou knowest that I can't hit or kick thee; but if thou kickest me one more time, I shall sell thee to a Baptist, and he shall kick the devil out of you."

The drought was so bad that the Baptists started to sprinkle, the Methodists used a wet rag, and the Presbyterians were giving rain checks.

A man was going to Rome and wanted to meet the Pope. A friend said, "Tell him some jokes." He met the Pope and asked him if he had heard about the two Polacks. The Pope said, "Wait a minute, I'm Polish." The man said, "That's all right. If you don't catch it the first time, I'll tell it again."

A little girl was out in the yard when it was lightning and thundering. Her mother called her into the house and asked her what she was doing outside in such bad weather. She answered, "God was taking my picture."

The teacher asked the students to bring in a show-and-tell project about their religion. The next morning the teacher asked, "Who is ready to share their project?" Johnnie got up and said, "I'm Johnnie, this is a crucifix, and I'm a Catholic." Elizabeth got up and said, "I'm Elizabeth, this is the Star of David, and I'm Jewish." James got up and said, "I'm James, this is a casserole, and I'm Baptist."

A man converted from Baptist to Catholic and went to see the priest for confession. The priest asked, "What have you done?" The man said, "I have sinned. I stole some lumber and built a doghouse." The priest said, "Well, that's not so bad." The man said, "Well, that's not all of it. I also built a two-car garage." The priest replied, "That's pretty bad." The man continued, "Well, that's not all of it either. I built a five-bedroom house." The priest said, "That's real bad. You will be required to make two novenas." The man said, "Well, if you can draw up the plans, I have the lumber to build them."

Christians are like tea bags; they're not worth much until they've been put through hot water.

The Pope was sick with bird flu—he caught it from one of his Cardinals.

A lady got up in church and said that there was a certain man in the church who was an alcoholic and needed to be dealt with. She said that she had seen his pickup in front of a bar several times, and she just knew he was an alcoholic. The man didn't say a word. The next night he parked his pickup in front of her house and left it there all night.

Three boys were bragging about their fathers. The first boy said, "My daddy scribbled a few words on a piece of paper, and they called it a poem and gave him $50." The second boy said, "That's nothing; my dad scribbled a few words on a piece of paper, and they called it a song and gave him $100." The third boy said, "I got you both beat. My dad scribbled some words on a piece of paper, and he called it a sermon. It took eight people to collect all the money."

A father was approached by his small son after Sunday School class, who told him proudly, "I know what the Bible means!" His father smiled and replied, "Okay, what does the Bible mean?" The son said, "That's easy, Daddy. It stands for Basic Information Before Leaving Earth."

A very gracious woman was mailing an old family Bible to her brother in another part of the country. "Is there anything breakable in here?" asked the postal clerk. "Only the Ten Commandments," answered the woman.

A grandfather was walking through his yard when he heard his granddaughter repeating the alphabet in a tone of voice that sounded like a prayer. He asked her what she was doing. The little girl explained, "I'm praying, but I can't think of exactly the right words. So I'm just saying all the letters, and God will put them together for me because He knows what I'm thinking."

The minister was preoccupied with thoughts of how he was going to ask the congregation to come up with more money that was needed for repairs to the church building. He was annoyed to find that the regular organist was sick, and a substitute was brought in at the last minute. The substitute wanted to know what to play. "Here's a copy of the service," he said impatiently, "but you'll have to think of something to play after I make the announcement about the finances."

During the service, the minister paused and said, "Brothers and sisters, we are in great difficulty; the roof repairs cost twice as much as we expected, and we need $4,000 more. Any of you who can pledge $100 or more, please stand up." At that moment, the substitute organist played "The Star Spangled Banner." That is how the substitute became the regular organist!

WORDS OF WISDOM

The tongue is the thermometer that tells the temperature of the person.

Church Folk

The Southern Ten Commandments

1. Y'all shalt always remember your manners.

2. Y'all shalt make no fuss over yourself.

3. Y'all shalt not sass your mama.

4. Y'all shalt always wonder what your daddy would think.

5. Y'all shalt always talk the way you growed up.

6. Y'all shalt tell no whoppers unless you are in a situation where you're expected to.

7. Y'all shalt demonstrate your great faith by the way you drive.

8. Y'all shalt always clean your plate.

9. Y'all shalt hold kinfolk in high regard, regardless of what you really think of 'em.

10. Y'all shalt always remember where you came from.

My wife talks 140 words
a minute with gusts
up to 180!

Love and Marriage

A man sent his picture to a Lonely Hearts Club. They sent it back and said, "We are not that lonely."

<hr/>

Boy to Girl: If you'll give me your phone number, I'll give you a call.
Girl: It's in the book.
Boy: What's your name?
Girl: It's in the book too.

<hr/>

Two old maids were excited about getting to go on a date. They agreed that when they came downstairs for breakfast the next morning at the boarding house that they would say "morning" for every time they were kissed on their date. The first one came in and said, "Good morning." The second one came in all smiles and said, "Good morning, this morning, fine morning this morning, if it is as pretty a morning in the morning as it is this morning, it will be a pretty morning in the morning."

⁓

One man told his friend, "My girl friend takes advantage of me." The friend asked, "What do you mean?" He replied, "I invited her out to dinner, and she asked if she could bring a date."

⁓

Love: A feeling you feel you're going to feel when you have a feeling you feel you haven't felt before.

⁓

Husband to wife: "Honey, I can tell you've lost weight."
Wife: "Yes, I'm finally down to what I should have never been up to in the first place."

⁓

A wife said to her husband, "When you were younger, you used to nibble on my ear." The husband started to leave the room, and his wife asked him where he was going. He said, "To get my teeth."

Joe: "My wife doesn't understand me. Does yours?"
Rob: "My wife doesn't even know you."

Two men were talking, and one said, "Every once in a while my wife puts on one of those mudpacks." The other man said, "Does it work?" The first man replied, "Only for two or three days, then the mud falls off."

A wife said: "Honey have you noticed how bald you're getting?" The husband replied: "I'm not getting bald; my hair is like the waves of the sea." The wife said, "Yes, but have you noticed that the tide is out?"

A husband said to his wife, "Honey, meet me at the Waldorf Astoria at 6 o'clock." The wife said, "My, my, that's a real nice place." The husband replied, "Yes, it's close to where we're going."

～

A man carried around pictures of all his children and a CD of his wife.

～

A man asked his friend, "How many years have you been married?" He said, "We've had 20 good years." The first man said, "I thought you'd been married 25 years." The friend said, "We have, but 20 out of 25 ain't bad."

～

This couple drove to Wal-Mart. When they arrived, their car broke down in the parking lot. The husband told his wife to go on ahead and do her shopping, and he'd fix the car.

She returned later to find a small group near the car. She observed a pair of legs sticking out from under the car and realized what was going on. Her husband was wearing shorts because it was a very hot day.

She was embarrassed for him and knew he would be also, so she stepped forward. Being modest, she tried to cover him up and tuck everything back in place.

Some disturbance caused her to leap to her feet, and she found herself looking right at her husband standing across the parking lot, watching everything. The mechanic, however, had to have three stitches in his head.

The best way to stay hitched is to have good horse sense, stable thinking, and a bridle on your tongue.

Words of Wisdom

Marriage: An investment that pays you dividends if you pay interest.

It got so hot
that all the cows were giving
evaporated milk!

Down on the Farm

A farmer held up his pigs to get apples off the tree. His friend said, "Look at the time you'd save if you just shook the tree." The farmer said, "Oh man, what's time to a hog?"

~~~~~~~~~

A chicken passed a car going down the road, ran off, and left the car. The man decided to follow it to the farmhouse. At the house, the man asked the farmer why the chicken had three legs. The farmer said, "They are bred that way because of the drumsticks." The man asked if the chicken's drumsticks taste good, and the farmer said, "We don't know, we haven't been able to catch one yet."

~~~~~~~~~

The farmer had a rooster that was so lazy he'd wait until all the other roosters crowed, then he would just nod his head in agreement.

These two old farmers were talking and bragging about their farms and how big they were. One said to the other, "I can get in my truck one morning, and when nighttime comes, I'm still on my property." The other one said, "That's nothing, I used to have an old truck like that too."

The city boy went to the country and asked Uncle George how long cows should be milked. Uncle George said, "The same as the short ones."

The farmer was working full speed ahead building a fence when his neighbor asked him why he was in such a hurry. He said, "I'm trying to get through before I run out of nails."

A farmer went to a horse auction to buy a horse. The horse trader said, "I have just the right one for you. It's three years old, in good health, and goes ten miles without stopping." The farmer said, "Well, I can't use him. I only live eight miles from town, and with that horse I'll have to walk back two miles."

The farmer asked his neighbor what happened to the other windmill he used to have. The neighbor said, "There was only enough wind for one, so we took it down."

***

You'll have to think on this one: A farmer was having a hard time telling his two horses apart. So he decided to measure them. He found out the black horse was two inches taller than the white one.

***

A farmer was leading his mule to town. His friend stopped and asked him if he wanted to ride. And he said, "Sure, my mule will follow; he knows the way to town." So the farmer got in the truck, and the mule began to follow. They sped up to 30 miles an hour, and the mule was right behind them. They sped up to 50 miles an hour, and the mule kept right up.

When they got up to 70 miles an hour, the friend looked into the rearview mirror. The mule was right in back of the truck with his eyes bulging and his tongue hanging out. The man said, "I can't believe it. He's still right behind us!"

The farmer asked, "Which side is his tongue hanging out on?" The friend replied, "The left side." Then the farmer said, "Keep in this lane—he's going to pass!"

~

A farmer and his son were in the field plowing, and a neighbor came by and said, "You need to send that boy to school and get him an education." So the farmer sent his son off to college. After he graduated, he was right back out in the field plowing.

The neighbor came by and said, "I thought you sent that boy to school. What's he doing out there plowing? What good did college do?" The farmer bragged, "You just listen to him talk to the mule when he gets to the end of the row. Before he went off to school, he would say, 'Whoa and get up!' Now when he gets to the end of the row, he says, 'Halt, pivot to the left, and proceed forward!'"

~

A Failure to Communicate

A farmer went to an attorney and said he wanted one of them divorces.

Attorney: "Do you have grounds?"

Farmer: "Yup, I got 30 acres."

Attorney: "No, that's not what I mean. I mean do you have a case?"

Farmer: "Nope, I got a John Deere. That's what I farm them 30 acres with."

Attorney: "No, you don't understand me. Do you want to bring suit? Have you got a grudge?"

Farmer: "Well, I got a suit at home in the closet; and as for a grudge, that's where I keep my John Deere."

Attorney: "Oh, we're not communicating at all. Let's talk about your wife for a minute. Do you beat her up?"

Farmer: "Nope, she gets up about 6:30, about the same time I do."

WORDS OF WISDOM

Sow a thought, reap an act; sow an act, reap a habit; sow a habit, reap a character; sow a character, reap a destiny.

My dad used to say, "Son,
I've told you two million times,
don't exaggerate!"

Growing Pains

When the baby was born, it was so big that he was born on the first, second, third, and fourth of July!

~~~

This one baby was so ugly that when he was born, the stork circled the house three times before he had the nerve to drop him off.

~~~

A little boy asked his dad, "How does an airplane stay up in the air? How does a big ship float? How does a train stay on a track?" His dad replied, "I don't know, son." The boy asked, "Do you ever get tired of my asking questions?" His dad said, "No, son, how else are you ever gonna learn?"

~~~

A teacher asked the class who wrote the Declaration of Independence. Everybody answered correctly but little Johnny, and he said, "I don't know, and I don't care." Finally, the teacher called Johnny's dad, and he came down and had a talk with Johnny. He told the boy to never get smart with the teacher, and if he had anything to do with writing that thing, he had better confess it right then.

A little boy was practicing hitting some baseballs. He would throw the ball up and swing at it. He did this several times and missed every ball. Finally, he threw it up one more time and missed it. Then he whistled and said, "Wow, what a pitcher!"

I stopped to watch a Little League game and asked one of the boys what the score was. He said, "It's fourteen to nothing, against us." He had a smile on his face, so I said, "You don't look discouraged at all." He said, "Why should I be? We haven't been to bat yet."

There are three ways to get something done: Do it yourself. Hire someone to do it. Forbid your kids to do it.

~~~

Two boys walking down the railroad track thought about catching a ride. One boy jumped onto the train and disappeared into an empty boxcar. The boys didn't see each other for about a month. Then the other boy asked his returning friend what had happened to him. The friend said that the boxcar didn't have a floor in it, and he had to run all the way to Tennessee.

~~~

A little boy came home from school and was crying. He said, "Mommy, they're calling me a three-headed monster at school." Then she replied, "Now there, there, there."

~~~

When a baby boy was born, the parents wanted to name him something different, so they named him Fantastic. He went all through life hating that name.

Near the end of his life, he became very ill and decided to make his final arrangements. He told everyone that he hated his name and did not want it on his tombstone. When he died, they buried him and on his tombstone was written: "Mr. Brown. He never looked at another woman." Now when people pass by the tombstone, they look at it and say, "That's Fantastic!"

A teacher told her students to come prepared the next day to tell a story. The first little boy said, "I'm ready with my story." The teacher told him to go ahead. He said, "Me and my daddy gathered up all the eggs and put them in a big basket in the back of the truck. We was taking them to town when we hit a bump, and it spilled all the eggs." The teacher asked, "What is the moral of the story?" He said, "Never put all your eggs in one basket."

A large woman waiting in a long line at the grocery store checkout counter had on a beeper that went off. A little boy who was waiting behind, looked up at his mama and said, "Look out, Mama, she's backing up!"

A boy put some Odor Eaters in his tennis shoes, and by the end of the day there was nothing left but a radio and sunglasses.

The teacher asked a little boy what his dad did for a living. He said, "He's a magician. His specialty is sawing people in two." The teacher asked, "Do you have any brothers and sisters?" "Yes," the little boy said, "one half brother and one half sister."

This bully in school was always beating me up and taking my lunch money. Finally, one day I said to her, "Don't you ever do that to me again."

Johnny asked his teacher if he would be punished for something he didn't do. The teacher said, "Why certainly not." Johnny said, "I haven't done my homework today."

Little Cecil went to the park with his parents, and they got separated. Cecil found a policeman and asked for help. The officer said, "I don't think I can help you, son, there are too many places for them to hide."

A little nine-year-old boy jumped up at the dinner table, hit his fist on the table, and said, "I hate string beans!" The mother said, "Son, you're nine years old, and you've never said a word in your life. We were so concerned about you. Why all of a sudden did you speak up?" He said, "Up till now, everything has been all right."

A new teacher was trying to make use of her psychology courses. She started her class by saying, "Everyone who thinks they're stupid, stand up!" After a few seconds, little Johnny stood up. The teacher said, "Do you think you're stupid, Johnny?" "No, ma'am, but I hate to see you standing there all by yourself!"

Little Johnny watched, fascinated, as his mother smoothed cold cream on her face. "Why do you do that, Mommy?" he asked. "To make myself beautiful," said his mother, who then began removing the cream with a tissue. "What's the matter?" asked Little Johnny. "Giving up?"

The math teacher saw that Johnny wasn't paying attention in class. She called on him and said, "Johnny! What are 2 and 4 and 28 and 44?" Little Johnny quickly replied, "NBC, FOX, ESPN, and the Cartoon Network!"

Little Johnny's kindergarten class was on a field trip to their local police station where they saw pictures tacked to a bulletin board of the ten most wanted criminals. One of the youngsters pointed to a picture and asked if it really was the photo of a wanted person. "Yes," said the policeman. "The detectives want very badly to capture him." Little Johnny asked, "Why didn't you keep him when you took his picture?"

A little boy dug a hole in his yard. When asked by his neighbor why he was digging a hole, he replied, "My goldfish died." The neighbor said, "Why are you digging such a large hole?" The boy answered, "It was in your cat!"

~~~

According to a radio report, a middle school in Oregon was faced with a unique problem. A number of girls were beginning to use lipstick and would put it on in the bathroom. That was fine, but after they put on their lipstick, they would press their lips to the mirror, leaving dozens of little lip prints.

Finally, the principal decided that something had to be done. She called all the girls to the bathroom and met them there with the maintenance man. She explained that all these lip prints were causing a major problem for the custodian, who had to clean the mirrors every night. To demonstrate how difficult it was to clean the mirrors, she asked the maintenance guy to clean one of them. He took out a long-handled squeegee, dipped it into the toilet, and then cleaned the mirror. Since then there have been no lip prints on the mirror.

I always wanted to be somebody, but I should have been more specific.

WORDS OF WISDOM
The two most important days of our lives are the day we are born and the day we find out why.

Trooper: "Boy, you got any I.D.?"
Redneck: "About what?"

Public Servants

A lady called the fire station and said that her house was on fire. The fire chief asked, "How do we get there?" She said, "Don't y'all still have those little red trucks?"

A man staggered out of the bar and out to the street. He was walking with one foot on the curb and one foot on the road when a policeman saw him, tapped him on the shoulder, and said, "You'll have to come with me—you are drunk." The man looked at him and said, "Thank God. I thought I was crippled."

I live in a bad neighborhood. The robbers work only in the daytime because they're afraid to be out on the street after dark. In fact, things are so bad that the police department has an unlisted number.

A boy was in the service, and his father wrote him a letter and told him to be good and have a good time. The boy wrote back and said, "Make up your mind!"

A redneck sheriff stopped a boy in a car on the back roads and told him to roll down his window and show him his driver's license. He asked the boy where he was from, and the boy said, "Chicago." The sheriff looked at the driver's license and said, "What are you doing with this Illinois driver's license, boy?"

A cop stopped a car and the man rolled down the window. The cop said, "Man, your eyes are red. Have you been drinking?" The man looked up at the cop and said, "Man, your eyes are glazed. Have you been eating doughnuts?"

A guy said, "My wife just got a ticket for speeding." His friend said, "That's nothing. My wife is so bad the police gave her a season ticket."

Interviewer to politician: "Sir, we only have a few minutes left. Could you briefly give us some idea of what you have been talking about for the past half hour?"

As the cop was helping the man off the sidewalk, he said, "Can you describe the man who hit you?" "Sir," he replied, "That's what I was doing when he hit me."

A traveler stopped to ask directions from a cop, "Is this the road to Memphis?" The cop said, "It depends on which way you're going."

A man fell out of a two-story window. When he hit the ground, a policeman ran over and said, "What's going on here?" The other man said, "I don't know; I just got here myself."

A young man who was having trouble getting anything to go right for him decided to join the Army. After a while, he was called in to participate in war games. He got in line to get his weapon, and when they got to him, they were out of weapons.

The supply sergeant said, "You take this broomstick and when you see the enemy you say, 'Bangety, bang, bang,' and they will fall over dead." So he headed out and saw a couple of enemies and said, "Bangety, bang, bang" and sure enough they fell over. He thought, *WOW this works pretty well.*

Then he saw another enemy coming his way, so he stepped out and said, "Bangety, bang, bang." The enemy kept coming at him. After he said it a couple more times, the enemy just ran right over him. The enemy looked back and said, "Tankety, tank, tank.

A state trooper was driving along a mountain road and saw an Indian lying with his ear to the ground. He heard him saying, "Chevy pickup, large tires, green, and man driving with large German Shepherd in passenger seat. Loaded with firewood, California license plate 1-896-PUC." The trooper asked, "You mean you can tell all that by listening to the ground?" "No," the Indian said. "A truck just ran over me."

<hr>

A woman was about to have a baby. The time came and the husband called 911. The lady tried to calm him down; then she asked him, "Is this her first child?" He said, "No, I'm her husband."

<hr>

A man found a monkey loose on the street. He picked him up, put him in his truck, and started down the street. A cop saw him and said, "Man, you ought to take him to the zoo." So the next day he was driving and the cop saw him again, "I thought you were gonna take him to the zoo." He said, "I did and we had so much fun that today we're going to the fair."

<hr>

A minister parked his car in a no-parking zone in a large city because he was short on time and couldn't find a space with a meter. Then he put a note under the windshield wiper that read: "I have circled the block ten times. If I don't park here, I'll miss my appointment. Forgive us our trespasses."

When he returned, he found a citation from a police officer along with this note, "I've circled this block for ten years. If I don't give you a ticket, I'll lose my job. Lead us not into temptation."

Two elderly people were pulled over by a policeman who demanded the husband's driver's license. The officer asked the man, "Do you know how fast you were going? What's your destination?"

The husband gave him his license and said, "We're going to Rustin, Louisiana."

The trooper said, "I knew a woman there who was so ugly, she could make a train go down a dirt road."

The wife, who could not hear very well, asked, "What did he say?" The husband replied, "He said he thinks he knows you."

A man found a body in New Orleans and called 911. The operator asked, "Where are you?" The man said, "I am on Thopatulas Street." She said, "Spell that for me."

He thought for a moment and then said, "Can I just drag him over to Oak Street, and you can pick him up there?"

WORDS OF WISDOM

You may be disappointed if you fail, but you are doomed if you don't try. Occasionally, failure is the price of improvement.

You can make a small fortune
gambling IF you start out
with a big one!

Money, Money, Money

Two men were talking. One said, "I'd give a hundred dollars if someone would do my worrying for me." The other man said, "You're on. Where is the hundred dollars?" The first man said, "That's your first worry."

~~~~~~

A man in the restaurant asked the waiter how much the average tip was. The waiter said, "$5." So the man finished his dinner and handed the waiter $5. The waiter looked shocked and surprised, so the man asked, "What's wrong? I thought you said the average tip was $5." The waiter replied, "Yes it is, but you're the first one to come up to the average."

~~~~~~

A man built a fine two-story house. While he was building it, it was one story and when he tried to pay for it, it was quite another story.

My dad said that there was money in eggs, so I broke every one we had. I can't figure it out—I never found a cent.

A man's father had died, and his son was going through his clothes and found a ticket for shoe repair from back in the '50s. Being a thrifty man, he set out to find the shop. When he got there, a little old man was at the counter. He showed him the ticket, and the little man said, "Yes, they will be ready on Tuesday."

It's hard to climb the ladder of success, especially if you're trying to keep your nose to the grindstone, your head above water, your shoulder to the wheel, your eyes on the ball, and your ear to the ground.

There were these two Indians who slept in the lobby of the hotel because they couldn't afford a reservation.

The best way to keep water out of your house is to not pay the bill.

When you're 30, you believe your thinking is so superior that you can create a way to get rich quick. By age 40, you hope to get rich gradually. When you're 50, you're thankful to keep up on the payments on your medical bills.

When we got married, we had nothing; we still have half of it.

Two cousins from Louisiana—Boudreaux and Thibodeaux—lost their job at a women's undergarment factory. At an interview for unemployment, Boudreaux was asked by the interviewer, "What did you do?" He said, "Sew elastic in women's under clothes." The interviewer said, "You get $150 for unskilled labor."

Then came Thibodeaux's turn. When he was asked, "What did you do?" he said, "I was a diesel fitter."

The interviewer said, "You get $300." Boudreaux became quite upset because his cousin received more money. He said all Thibodeaux did was to hold the undergarments up and say, "Dees'll fit her."

⌖

A $1 bill says to a $20 bill, "Where have you been?" The $20 bill says, "Everywhere, having a good time. Where have you been?" The $1 bill says, "Church, church, church is all I ever do.'

⌖

A stingy old lawyer who was diagnosed with a terminal illness didn't believe the saying, "You can't take it with you." So he told his wife to go down to the bank, fill up a pillowcase full of money, and put it directly over his bed in the attic. When he died, he could grab the money on his way up to heaven.

Well, after he died, his wife was cleaning the attic and found the money still there. She said, "I knew all along I should have put that money in the basement."

⌖

A gorilla walked into a drug store and ordered a $1 milkshake and put $10 on the counter. The clerk thought to himself, *What does a gorilla know about money*, so he gave him $1 back in change. The clerk said, "You know we don't get many gorillas in here." The gorilla said, "It's no wonder at $9 a milkshake."

My wife just had plastic surgery. I cut up all her credit cards.

Here is a surefire way to double your money: fold it in half and put it in your pocket.

A man down in the tropical islands sent a bird to his dad back in the States. A week later he called his dad and asked, "Dad, did you get the bird?" His dad said, "Yes, I did." The son said, "Well, how did you like him?" The dad said, "I really did like him; he was delicious." The son said, "Dad, you surely didn't eat him. He cost me $5000, and he could speak five languages." The dad said, "Well, he should have said something."

This one woman was so big that she had to buy group insurance.

The preacher said, "Everyone should give one tenth to the Lord." A little ole man in the back said, "Amen and let's raise it to one twentieth."

Some people are so poor they can't even pay attention. Being poor is one thing money can't buy.

A woman was diagnosed with sclerosis of the giver, which greatly hindered her reach, so she went to the hospital and had her tithe removed.

My wife is just impossible; she is always asking for money. Last week she asked for $100, earlier this week she asked for $200, and this morning she asked for $300. A friend said, "My, that's a lot of money. What does she do with all of it?" The husband said, "I don't know; I never give her any."

One man asked God how long a million years was to Him. God said, "A million years is like a minute." The man asked God what a million dollars was to Him and God said, "A million dollars is like a penny." Then the man asked God if he could have a penny, and God said, "In a minute."

WORDS OF WISDOM

God owns the cattle on 1,000 hills. What He needs are some good cowboys to help round them up.

When your outgo exceeds your inflow, your overhead becomes your downfall.

Always smile; it increases your face value.

This one dog was so lazy that he would not chase cars. He'd just lie by the side of the road and take tag numbers.

Strange Critters

A woman bought a parrot that cussed like a sailor. She decided to break the bird from cussing. She told him she would put him in the refrigerator every time he cussed. She did so several times, leaving him in there a little longer each time.

The last time he ever cussed, she left him in there a real long time. He came out shaking his feathers all over. He said, "I've got one question. What did that turkey say?"

~~~

An atheist was spending a quiet day fishing when suddenly the Loch Ness monster attacked his boat. In one easy flip, the beast tossed him and his boat high in the air, then opened its mouth to swallow them.

As the man sailed head over heals, he cried out, "Oh my God, help me!" At once, the ferocious attack scene froze in place. As the atheist hung in mid-air, a booming voice came from the clouds, "I thought you didn't believe in Me."

"Come on, God, give me a break," the man pleaded. "Two minutes ago I didn't believe in the Loch Ness monster either."

A man was standing on a street corner, swinging a chain, when his friend came up and asked him what he was doing. He said that he was keeping the elephants away. The friend said, "Ah, man, you know there ain't any elephants within a 100 miles from here." Then the man replied, "See there—it works, doesn't it?"

A salesman came up to a house with a woman and dog on the front porch. He asked the woman if her dog would bite. She said, "No." So he climbed up the stairs. The dog jumped on him, bit him, and scratched him all over. He complained to the woman, "I thought you said your dog wouldn't bite." She said, "That's not my dog."

Two cows were standing out in the pasture one day and saw a milk truck pass by. Printed on its side were the words, "Pasteurized, homogenized, and pure." One cow looked at the other and said, "It kinda makes you feel inadequate, doesn't it?"

A guy walked into a store with a duck under his arm. The clerk said, "Where did you get that pig?" The guy said, "That's not a pig; that's a duck." The clerk said, "I was talking to the duck."

This clothing store had one suit that never would sell, so one day the owner told the salesman that he was taking a long lunch break, and he wanted the suit sold by the time he came back.

Two hours later the owner came back and found the salesman all scratched up and his clothes torn in pieces. He said, "Well, did you sell that suit?" The salesman said, "Yes." The owner said, "Did he like it?" The salesman said, "Yes, he did, but his Seeing Eye dog didn't like it at all."

This one fellow thought he saw light at the end of the tunnel and found out it was a grizzly bear with a flashlight.

~~~

A man and wife went into the pet store. A parent in the cage at the front of the store said, "Hey." The man said, "What?" The parrot said, "That's the ugliest woman I ever saw."

It made the man furious, so he went to the manager and told him the parrot had greatly insulted his wife. The manager told the parrot, "If you ever say anything to insult a customer again, you are out of here."

So the couple shopped around a while and then headed to the front. As they passed by, the parrot said, "Hey." The man said, "What?" The parrot said, "You KNOW what."

~~~

WORDS OF WISDOM

Never tell a bird he can't fly when he is in midair.

He was a self-made man
and worshipped his creator.

Even Stranger Folk

There was a crazy man who came knocking at a door at 3 a.m., waking a couple up. The man of the house went and opened the door. The man standing on the outside said, "I need a push."

The sleepy man quickly shut the door in his face and went back to bed. His wife said, "Honey do you remember the time we needed a push and someone came to help us?"

Feeling badly, the man got back up and went back to the door, but he couldn't see the crazy guy. So he called out, "Where are you? Are you out here?" And a man's voice came from a swing out in the yard saying, "I need a push."

They decided to throw me a big birthday party one year. They called all of my friends but neither one of them could come!

Two hippies woke up in the hospital. One looked at the other and said, "Man, didn't you see that wall?" The other said, "I saw the wall, but I didn't know I was driving."

Two soldiers were talking. One said, "This pie tastes like glue." His buddy said, "It's apple; the pumpkin tastes like soap."

So far today I've done all right. I haven't gossiped. I haven't lost my temper. I haven't been greedy, grumpy, nasty, selfish, or overindulgent. I'm really glad about that. But in a few minutes, God, I'm going to get out of bed. From then on, I'm probably going to need a lot more help.

A fellow came up to a man on the street and asked if he wanted to be a Jehovah Witness. The man said, "I didn't even see the accident."

A funeral procession was carrying a casket to the grave site for a funeral. When they went around a corner the back door came open, the casket came out, slid across the street and through the door of a pharmacy. The lid flew open, and the man sat up and said, "You got anything to stop this coffin?"

Two men met on the street and one said to the other, "You are Tom Jones; of course you've lost weight and don't have as much hair." The other man said, "I'm Frank Smith." Then the first one replied, "Yes and you changed your name too."

I'm in good shape. Round is a shape, isn't it?

A man saw his friend going down the street, pulling a chain. He asked him, "Why are you pulling that chain?" His answer was, "Have you ever tried pushing one?"

This man predicted the world would end in 1697. In 1698, he wrote another book that it did end, but nobody noticed.

～～～

A woman came up to the checkout counter and asked if she could buy half a head of cabbage because she couldn't afford a whole head. The checkout boy said, "I don't know, I'll go ask the manager."

Without his knowledge, the woman followed him. He told the manager, "There's some idiot up there who wants to buy half a head of cabbage." Then he noticed the woman was right behind him and said, "And this nice lady wants to buy the other half."

～～～

The manager said, "Son, you are a quick thinker— where are you from?" He said, "I'm from Lancaster, Pennsylvania, where there are only hockey players and ugly women."

The manager said, "Wait a minute, my wife is from there." And the boy said, "What team does she play on?"

One afternoon, a wealthy lawyer was riding in the back of his limousine when he saw two men eating grass by the roadside. He ordered his driver to stop, and he got out to investigate.

"Why are you eating grass?" he asked one man. "We don't have any money for food," the poor man replied. "Oh, come along with me then," instructed the lawyer. "But, sir, I have a wife and two children!" the man said. "Bring them along!" replied the lawyer.

He turned to the other man and said, "Come with us." "But, sir, I have a wife and six children!" the second man protested. "Bring them as well!" said the lawyer as he headed for his limo.

They all climbed into the car, which was no easy task, even for a car as large as a limo. Once underway, one of the poor fellows said, "Sir, you are too kind. Thank you for taking all of us with you." The lawyer replied, "No problem, the grass at my home is almost a foot tall."

A slightly large lady went into a bank in northern Mississippi. At the front was a newfangled scale with a robotic voice that spoke out how much you weigh. This lady got in line behind a man and woman to try it out. When the man got on the scale, it said, "One hundred ninety-two pounds." Next the woman got on and it said, "One hundred twenty-four pounds." When the large lady stepped on the scale, a voice boomed out, "One at a time, please!"

⤜∽∽⤛

There is an oil and gas shortage in this country. The only problem is that we can't check the oil because all the oil is in Texas, and all the dipsticks are in Washington.

⤜∽∽⤛

A dwarf bought a pair of cowboy boots and then couldn't wear them because he couldn't bend his knees.

⤜∽∽⤛

This woman had three sons. One gave her a new house, one gave her a new car, and one gave her a parrot to read the Bible to her. She said, "The house is too big, the car is too big, but that was the best chicken I ever had."

~~~~~~

A new maid came for the first time to clean house. The housewife said, "I can write my name in the dust on the piano." The maid said, "Oh my, it must be wonderful to have an education."

~~~~~~

One man to another: "I am a light eater—when it gets light, I start eating."

~~~~~~

A ship captain had worked his way up through the ranks and become successful. One of his young sailors decided to watch him closely and follow him around to learn how he became successful.

After several months of watching, he determined that the captain went to his cabin every morning, got a piece of paper out, read it, and then went on with his day. One morning the young sailor decided to look and see what was on the paper. It read, "Port is on the left, Starboard on the right."

$$\sim$$

Two old ladies were talking. "An issue came up recently," one said. "Some of our friends were for it and some against it. We decided to stick with our friends."

$$\sim$$

Two men were talking and one asked the other, "What were you doing at 6 a.m. when the earthquake happened?" The other man said, "I was giving my wife instructions for the day. It scared me half to death and almost woke up my wife."

$$\sim$$

Being flexible means you can put either foot in your mouth.

$$\sim$$

A fellow riding in a taxi reached up and tapped the driver on the shoulder to ask him a question. The driver went wild, ran off the road and down into a ditch. The passenger said, "Why did you do that?" The driver said, "Well, this is my first day driving a taxi; up until now I have been driving a hearse."

Three men were going before a firing squad. The first one yelled, "Tornado!" Everyone scattered and he went free. The next one yelled, "Hurricane!" Everyone scattered and he went free. The final man thought about it and finally yelled, "Fire!"

An elderly lady died last month. Having never married, she requested no male pallbearers. In her handwritten instructions for her memorial service she wrote, "They wouldn't take me out when I was alive; I don't want them to take me out when I'm dead."

A man landed on planet with nothing but tall women. He got off the spaceship, went up to one of the women, and said, "Take me to your ladder, lady. I'll see your leader later."

The weatherman finally had to move because the weather would not agree with him.

$\sim$

A man's life is made up of 20 years of his mother asking where he's going and the next 30 to 50 years of his wife asking where he's been. Then one hour at his funeral, everyone wonders where he'll end up.

$\sim$

There is a new solution out for bald heads. It is a mixture of lemon juice and alum. It won't grow any hair, but it will shrink your head to match what you do have.

$\sim$

A woman got on the plane with a baby. There was a parrot on the plane that said, "That is the ugliest baby I have ever seen." The woman was furious.

She was so mad she turned red in the face and grumbled as she sat down next to a man. The man could see that she was mad about something because she kept saying that she was going to see the captain.

After a while, the man said to her, "You go ahead and talk to the captain. I'll hold your monkey for you."

WORDS OF WISDOM

A fanatic is someone who redoubles his efforts after he's lost his sense of vision.

Humor is funny business. It'll get them laughing. Then you can hit them in the teeth without bustin' their lip.

Prayer is asking for rain.
Faith is taking an umbrella!

The Good Book Says...

Who was the first comedian in the Bible? Samson. He brought the house down. Who was the first druggie in the Bible? Nebuchadnezzar? He was on grass.

◦～〜〜〜◦

Isaiah rode a mule named Isme. As he was riding along one day and his saddle came loose, he hollered out, "Whoa Isme for I am undone."

◦～〜〜〜◦

The Bible talks a lot about sports. It starts off talking about baseball, in the big inning. Then David must have played tennis because it says that he served in Saul's court. It also mentions football when it describes Moses being left back in Egypt.

What kind of man was Boaz before he got married?
He was Ruthless.

Worry is like a rocking chair—it gives you something to do, but it won't get you anywhere!

Don't worry about anything—pray about everything.
Thank God for anything.

Sin will always take you where you don't want to go,
keep you longer than you want to stay, and cost you
more than you want to pay.

People want the front of the bus, the back of the
church, and the center of attention.

Somebody has well said there are only two kinds of people in the world: There are those who wake up in the morning and say, "Good morning, Lord." Then there are those who wake up in the morning and say, "Good Lord, it's morning."

We are human beings not human doers. What we are speaks so loud that people can't hear what we are saying.

We should live our lives in such a way that we wouldn't mind selling our parrot to the town gossip.

If you are looking for the light at the end of the tunnel, then maybe you are looking in the wrong direction.

A good prescription for life is to
Live well, love much, and laugh a lot!

"Hello, I'm, I'm...
forgive me, I'm terrible
with names."

About the Author

Horace Vinson is overseer of Worship Center, Pascagoula, Mississippi, and Worship Center East in Grand Bay, Alabama, and a pastor of pastors. He was born in the area of Tupelo, Mississippi, and raised on a farm where he had a happy childhood. He spent four years in the military and has been a pastor for more than thirty-five years.

The author believes that laughter originated with God and is among the greatest gifts He has given to mankind. "He that sits in the heavens shall laugh," says the Psalmist.

To contact the author, email him at:
titus2wom@aol.com.